caillou® Concept Book

ABCs for Caillou and Me!

Modern Publishing
A Division of Unisystems, Inc.
New York, New York 10022
Printed in India
Series UPC: 19750

Learn the alphabet with Caillou!

A is for...

Apple

Airplane

Accordion

B is for...

Breakfast

Ball

Book

Bubbles

C is for...

Cape

Crawl

Cat

Coins

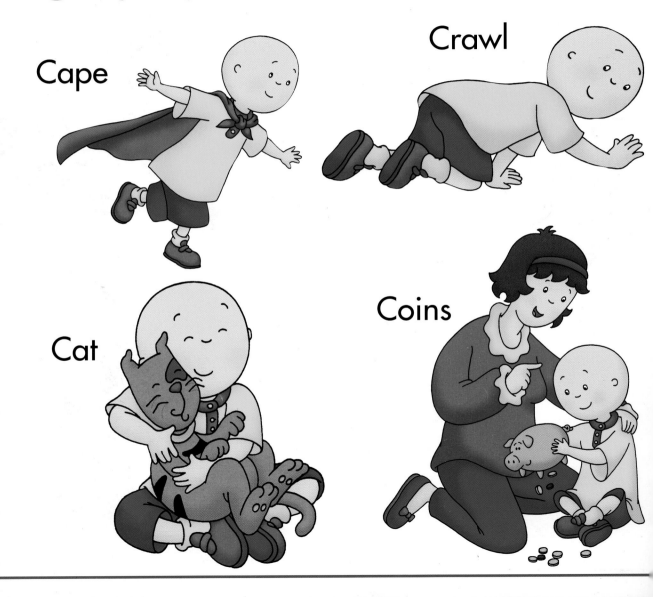

D is for...

Daddy

Dig

Dog

Drums

E is for...

Exercise

Explorers

Eggs

F is for...

Football

Flowers

Fishing

Flute

G is for...

Gift

Golf

Gilbert

Guitar

H is for...

Hopscotch

Hug

Harmonica

Helmet

I is for...

Ice Cream

Ice Skates

J is for...

Jacket

Jump

K is for...

Kite

Knee

Kitchen

L is for...

Lunch

Leaves

Laughter

Luggage

M is for...

Mirror

Mail

Marbles

O is for...

On

Orange

P is for...

Puddle

Puzzle

Puppets

Pillow

Q is for...

Quiet

R is for...

Rain

Roller Skates

S is for...

Soccer

Strawberries

Sled

T is for...

Telephone

Tiptoe

Toothbrush

Teddy Bear

U is for...

Upside-down

Umbrella

V is for...

Violin

W is for...

Wave

Wagon

Wheelbarrow

Watermelon

Winter

Write

X is for...

Xylophone

Y is for...

Yawn

Yo-Yo

Z is for...

Zebra